Gary Jones

Oslo

First published by Gary Jones in 2017

Copyright © Gary Jones, 2017

All rights reserved. No part of this publication may be reproduced, stored, or transmitted in any form or by any means, electronic, mechanical, photocopying, recording, scanning, or otherwise without written permission from the publisher. It is illegal to copy this book, post it to a website, or distribute it by any other means without permission.

*This book was professionally typeset on Reedsy.
Find out more at reedsy.com*

Contents

Introduction	1
Brief History and Background	4
Best Time to Go and Weather	12
Transportation	19
Top 5 Affordable Hotels	32
Top 5 Restaurants	37
Best Famous Oslo City Landmarks	42
Best Museums	52
Best Art Galleries	59
Best Coffee Shops	65
Top 5 Bars	68
Top 5 Nightclubs	72
Unique or Special Activities You can do Only in Oslo	76
Safety While Traveling in Oslo	84
3-Day Travel Itinerary	86
Conclusion	95

1

Introduction

Most people know that Oslo is the Scandinavian country of Norway's capital city. However, not all people know that Oslo has plenty of attractions to offer the adventurous local and international traveler.

Surrounded by hills, forests, and lakes, Oslo can be considered an undiscovered gem. Oslo is not as well-traveled as metropolitan areas like Paris, New York, or London, or even fellow Scandinavian cities like Stockholm or Copenhagen. Nevertheless, travelers to Norway – at some point – will pass through Oslo. And those who have done so will leave the city pleasantly surprised.

You won't be coming to Oslo to soak under the sun. Instead, you'll be coming here for winter- or nature-related activities. The city is also close to nature as its parks and countryside offer opportunities for cycling, hiking, boating, and skiing.

Like any other city in the world, Oslo allows you to indulge in activities like dining at restaurants, seeing city landmarks, and visiting museums and art galleries. Oslo's architectural landmarks are also extraordinary.

When you're not touring the city and its outskirts, you can relax at any of its coffee shops, bars, and nightclubs. There are also other activities that you can experience only in this bustling Norwegian city.

Oslo is indeed an easy-going metropolis with an atmosphere that is friendly to families. It's also a progressive city with a vibrant gay scene. Cultural activities and the nightlife scene are diverse. In short, Oslo offers a wide range of attractions to match your personal interests and tastes.

2

Brief History and Background

Oslo's documented history dates back to around 1000 CE. Since the Medieval times, Oslo has undergone multiple changes, including several name changes, too.

Oslo, which is the city's current name, was also the city's first name. During the Medieval times, the settlement was located east of the Bjørvika inlet. King Christian IV, after a fire in 1624, had the town rebuilt in an area underneath the Akershus Fortress. He then renamed Oslo to Christiania. It then reverted to the present name – Oslo – in 1925.

Oslo in the Middle Ages

The first town-like settlement may have been built around 1000 CE. Medieval Oslo was located between the Ekeberg hills, on the Bjørvika inlet's east side. Around 1300 CE, the town had about 3,000 inhabitants. King Haakon V, who reigned from 1299 to 1319, had commissioned the construction of the Akershus Fortress.

In the Old Town (Gamlebyen), you'll see medieval Oslo's cultural layers, building parts, and ruins. The old town is also the location of Oslo Ladegård's Medieval Office, which is an information office that sets up guided tours of the old town. Nearby is the memorial park with ruins of the St. Olav convent and the 12th century St. Hallvard cathedral.

Renaissance Oslo

In 1536, Norway united with Denmark. After the 1624 fire, King Christian IV of Denmark ordered the new settlement to be built below the Akershus Fortress. You can also find several well-preserved 17th-century buildings in Oslo. In Kvadraturen, you can see Oslo's old town hall as well as Café Engebret, which is the city's oldest restaurant.

The New Capital

In 1814, Denmark ceded Norway to King Karl Johan of Sweden. Norway then had its own constitution. On May 17, 1814, Christiania (renamed Oslo in 1925) became Norway's capital. In 1825, King Karl Johan started building the Royal Palace, which was completed in 1848 during King Oscar I's reign. The Parliament (Storting) building in Karl Johans gate was completed in 1866.

The industrial age in Norway started in 1850. Between 1850 and 1900, Christiania's population surged from around 30,000 to 230,000, due to an influx of rural-based workers.

A City Steeped in History

Oslo has undergone major changes because of redevelopment and fires, and most of the original town is gone. In certain neighborhoods, however, you can still get a sense of the past.

The Akershus Fortress for example, which has stood for over 700 years, is a vital cultural landmark. Many Norwegian patriots during

World War II were executed here, and the fortress was ceded to the Norwegian resistance movement in the war's final moments. Vidkun Quisling, after the war, was imprisoned in the fortress. Norway's Resistance Museum is also located within the fortress grounds.

Frogner Park is where you'll find the Oslo City Museum. The museum presents photos, objects, and models that put together a comprehensive picture of cultural and commercial activities, city development, and street life through the city's lengthy history.

The Akerselva River was Norway's cradle of industrialization. Walking along the river can be a pleasant experience, with old wooden houses and water cascades contrasting with massive industrial buildings.

BRIEF HISTORY AND BACKGROUND

3

Best Time to Go and Weather

The best time to go to Oslo is from May to September. During such time, the temperature averages around 15°C and there about 10 days of rain during September.

The late spring to summer to early autumn months may be the

time when you can experience milder temperatures. It may get chilly, though, so it's important to bring along a coat. Despite the temperature changes, Oslo offers the adventurer year-round activities. Let's see what every season has to offer for the Oslo visitor.

Oslo Temperatures

Winter (November to March)
Average Temperature: 0.7°C to 4.3°C
Lowest Temperature: -15.3°C
Maximum Temperature: 13.2°C

Spring (April to May)
Average Temperature: 4.5 to 10.8°C
Lowest Temperature: 2.4°C
Maximum Temperature: 25.2°C

Summer (June to August)
Average Temperature: 15.2°C to 16.4°C
Lowest Temperature: 6.1°C
Maximum Temperature: 30.5°C

Autumn (September to October)
Average Temperature: 6.3°C to 10.8°C
Lowest Temperature: 0.2°C
Maximum Temperature: 22.5°C

Set on the same latitude as most of Siberia and Alaska, Norway (including Oslo) has four distinct seasons, with each season having its character and benefits of visiting. Due to the Gulf Stream's warm air currents, temperatures tend to be more pleasant in the country's south than in the country's north.

Winter

In November, which is the start of the Norwegian winter, temperatures can drop considerably. The season is characterized by bitter cold and the lack of daylight. While snow can cover most of northern Norway, snow rarely settles along the southern coastal cities and towns – including Oslo.

At this point, Oslo can be an excellent starting off point if you want to go to areas having winter attractions. Norway then becomes a winter wonderland with excellent dog-sledging, skiing, snowmobiling, and ice fishing opportunities. In Oslo, you can still enjoy snow sports as there's a ski resort within the city's limits.

While it's cheaper to go to Norway during the winter, services are reduced. Thus, you need to plan for contingencies and plan your trip well if you seek to visit the country during this time. Precipitation comes down as snow from December to February.

Spring

As temperatures become warmer, the flowers start to bloom; the snow melts, and daytime become longer. Spring is graced with light showers, and the snow starts to melt during March. Spring is a wonderful time to visit the green landscapes, flowering orchards, and swollen waterfalls.

During April, there can be nightly subzero temperatures, which can cause melted snow to refreeze – leading to potentially dangerous road conditions. While early spring can be chilly, late spring can reach temperatures of 14°C.

Summer

When the sun is out during summers in Oslo, temperatures in the low 20s can be enjoyed immensely. The warmest months are August and July with temperatures in the low 20s. The temperatures rarely rise up to the 30s, and the nightly temperature usually dips to the teens.

During summers, you can do pretty much anything, except ski. You can hike through the woods, head out into the city, see the old city of Oslo, enjoy shopping, attend an outdoor concert, or indulge in the vibrant nightclub scene.

The winds blowing in from the Atlantic can make the summers unpredictable. You may end up visiting a sunny Oslo or a wet one with frequent rains. Rainfall increases during the start of summer and peaks in August.

The amount of daylight is one of the best things about the Norwegian summer. In June, there are around 5 hours between sunset and sunrise. While swimming in 17°C waters (even during summer) is not pleasant for most people, there are others who seek the cold and just jump right in.

Autumn

The season is wet and cold, and temperatures drop quickly. Days are becoming short. Autumn temperatures drop from 14°C in September to 7°C in October. Frost develops at night at the beginning of October, and there's a lot of rainfall during the season. It may get too cold, and rain can turn to snow. The average temperature at the end of autumn is about −1°C.

Autumn is also a good time to enjoy outdoor activities, as the countryside and forests turn into vibrant shades of orange and red. Wild fruit is ripest at September and crab is at its prime. Autumn is best for photography aficionados who want to capture the change in seasons. Foodies can also find autumns in Oslo appealing.

4

Transportation

Oslo's city center is small and can be navigated on foot. The suburbs, however, fan out to great distances, which warrants a metro-wide integrated public transportation system that consists of metro, trains, and buses to help you navigate the city and the surrounding counties.

Oslo Map
https://goo.gl/maps/LehMya4mqER2

Ruter AS coordinates public transport in Oslo and the nearby Akershus County, and individual operators are contracted to run specific services. Ruter controls pricing, planning, and managing the entire transport system. Ruter's tickets are valid for trams, buses, subways, local trains, and ferries (excluding the Bygdøy ferry).

Transfers to and From Gardermoen International Airport

The FlyToget train is the fastest way to and from the Oslo Airport in Gardermoen. In 19 minutes, FlyToget's shuttles connect the airport to the central station in Oslo.

Gardermoen International Airport Website
https://avinor.no/en/airport/oslo-airport/
Gardermoen International Airport Map
https://goo.gl/maps/7DawRRjUJcM2
Phone:+47 64 81 20 00

FlyToget Train Website
http://www.flytoget.no/flytoget_eng
Phone:+47 23 15 90 00
e-mail:flytoget@flytoget.no

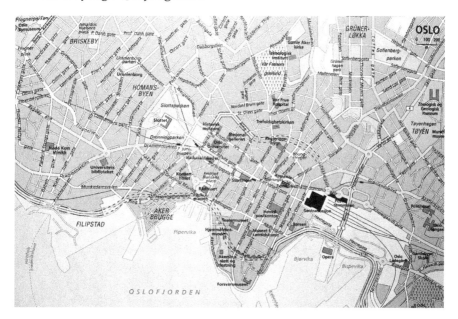

Between 4:40 am and midnight, trains depart every 10-20 minutes. Certain trains end at the central station, while others travel further to the National Theatre and stop south, ending at Drammen.

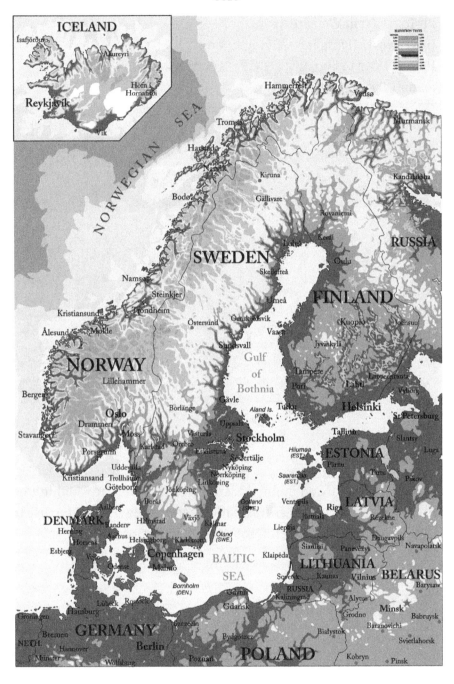

If you're traveling on a budget, you can ride the standard NSB (Norwegian State Railways) intercity and local train services that stop at Gardermoen (NOK90 for 26 minutes). One Norwegian Krone (NOK) is approximately $0.12 or (€)0.11. From the city, you can ride the trains at certain central stations including Oslo S. and Nationalteatret. The price is half that of FlyToget, and nearly as fast. However, NSB doesn't run as frequently as FlyToget.

Norwegian State Railways Website(NSB)
https://www.nsb.no/en/frontpage
Phone: 815 00 888 / (+47) 61 05 19 10

The equivalent of NSB, Flybussen, departs from the Gardermoen airport and ends at the Galleri Oslo terminal. It also serves few other city stops every 20 minutes from 4:00 am to about 10:00 pm. The trip from the airport, which takes about 40 minutes, costs NOK160 for adults and NOK80 for children.

Transfers to and from Torp Airport

Ryanair and other budget aircraft' flights land at Sandefjord Airport, Torp in Sandefjord, Norway. In around 110 minutes, the Torp-Expressen bus runs from the airport to the terminal in Galleri Oslo. Buses depart Oslo around 3 ½ hours before the closing of check-in. The buses leave the airport around 35 minutes after the arrival of a flight. However, the bus will wait for the plane that arrives late.

Torp Airport Website
http://www.torp.no/en/frontpage/
Torp Airport Map
https://goo.gl/maps/34XX8XTL2Rz

Torp-Expressen Website
http://torpekspressen.no/
Phone:+47 67 98 04 80

With a cost of NOK266, NSB trains run about every hour between Oslo S and Torp station. A shuttle bus converges with the trains and transports passengers to the airport. The fee for the shuttle ride is included in the train ticket price.

Oslo Pass

The Oslo Pass allows unlimited travel by tram, bus, underground, local train, and boat with NSB and Ruter, within zones 1 and 2. The Pass can also be used to travel to Drøbak (south), Lillestrøm (east), or Asker (west).

Night Buses. The Pass can be used on zones 1 and 2 night buses which run from 1:00 am to 4:00 am on Saturdays and Sundays.

Night Buses Oslo Website
https://ruter.no/en/journey-planner/night-buses/

Tusenfryd Amusement Park. Pass holders have complimentary transport to the amusement park, which is set in zone 2.

Ferries/Boats. The Pass can be used on the boats to Asker, Drøbak, and Nesodden. It can also be used on the ferries going to the Oslo Fjord islands and on the boats to Bygdøy.

Ferries Website
https://ruter.no/en/journey-planner/route-maps/

Ruter

Metro

Ruter is Oslo's main public transport system. It also serves the nearby county of Akershus. Ferries (excluding the Bygdøy ferry), local trains, metro/subway, trams, regional buses, and city buses are included in the Ruter ticket system.

Ruter Website (,trams,Metro,buses,ferries,trains)
https://ruter.no/en/

Tickets can be bought at any Ruter sales point. These places include 7-Eleven and Narvesen shops and metro stations' ticket machines. You should pre-purchase a ticket if you travel by tram or metro/subway.

Single Pre-Bought Ticket
Adult: NOK32
Senior/Child: NOK16

Single Ticket (Purchased from Driver)
Adult: NOK50
Senior/Child: 25NOK
One-Day Ticket
Adult: NOK90
Senior/Child: NOK45

7-Day Ticket
Adult: NOK240
Senior/Child: NOK120

30-Day Ticket
Adult: NOK690
Senior/Child: NOK345

Norwegian Student: NOK414
Year-Round Ticket
Adult: NOK6,900
Senior: NOK3,450

Norwegian State Railways (NSB)

NSB is Norway's national railway company and offers train services in Norway and between Gothenburg, Sweden, and Oslo. Many regional trains have complimentary wireless internet. To use it, however, you need to register.

Norwegian State Railways (NSB) Website
https://www.nsb.no/en/frontpage

The Ferries
Oslo Ferries (Boat to the Islands). The City Hall Pier 4 (Rådhusbrygge 4) boats take you to the inner Oslo Fjord islands. The ferries, during summer, operate from early in the morning to late at night. During winter, there are only 7 to 8 daily departures.

Ruter tickets can be used to board the ferries. However, tickets should be bought in advance as they are not available on the islands.

Bygdøyfergene (Boat to the Museums). You can use the Oslo Pass to board the Bygdøy ferries, which operate from March to October. The ferries depart every 20 to 30 minutes from Pier 3, which is located near City Hall.

One of the ferries' stops is Dronningen, which is the location of Oscarshall, Viking Ship Museum, and Norwegian Museum of Cultural History/Folk Museum). Another stop is Bygdøynes, the location of the Norwegian Maritime Museum, Fram, and Kon-Tiki.

When not using the Oslo Pass, you can buy tickets at Båtservice ticket office at Pier 3. The cost for a one-way ticket is NOK40, and the return ticket is NOK60. If you buy tickets on board, it costs NOK60.

Bicycle Rental

Bicycle Rental Website
http://www.vikingbikingoslo.com/en/
Bicycle Rental Map
https://goo.gl/maps/fCPzY25oAbx
Address:Nedre Slottsgate 4, 0157 Oslo
Phone:+47 412 66 496

TRANSPORTATION

5

Top 5 Affordable Hotels

Oslo is a compact city, as compared to capitals of other countries. In the city center, you can reach point A to point B in a relatively short amount of time. From the Oslo Central Station to the Royal Palace (via Karl Johan Street) it will only take about 15 minutes by walking.

If you want to go to the places beyond the city center, you can use public transport and easily reach popular tourist destinations like Bygdøy and Holmenkollen. Using the metro, it takes only 25 minutes to reach Holmenkollen from the city center. During the summer, it takes a 15-minute ferry ride to reach Bygdøy.

Each area in Oslo has unique characteristics. It's also no surprise the city is dotted with hotels, which are strategically located near metro stations so you can reach out-of-the-way destinations in a short amount of time. Some of the best budget hotels in Oslo are listed below.

Oslo Apartments – Sven Bruns Gate

This 3-star hotel/serviced apartment is located in Sven Bruns Gate 7 in Frogner, and is a 10-minute walk away from the Nationaltheatret Tram Station. The hotel is also a family-friendly serviced apartment.

Throughout the property, guests can enjoy the complimentary wireless internet. Each of the apartments features an in-room dining area, a coffee maker, and a refrigerator. The apartments also have ironing facilities, flat screen TVs, and seating areas.

The area where the hotel's at is known for its vibrant nightlife. Guests are spoilt for choice when it comes to bar and dining options. The Oslo Apartments – Sven Bruns Gate is also near the Homansbyen Light Rail Station, making it easy for visitors explore the city and the surrounding vicinity. Also near the hotel are Bislett Stadion and Oslo City Hall.

Oslo Apartments – Sven Bruns Gate Website
http://osloapartments.no/en/apartments-for-rent/oslo-central/sven-bruns-gate-7.html

Oslo Apartments – Sven Bruns Gate Map
https://goo.gl/maps/KE422GisX5R2
Address: Sven Bruns gate 7, 0166 Oslo, Norway
Phone:(+47) 22 51 02 50

Radisson Blu Plaza Hotel Oslo

This stylish 4-star hotel is located at Sonja Henies Plass 3 in Sentrum. The hotel is also set amid various boutiques and shops, and is minutes away from Bussterminalen Oslo.

As a guest, you can enjoy a sauna and an indoor pool. The hotel is also close to bars and clubs, and you can explore easily the local nightlife. One well-known landmark is the Oslo Spektrum, which is only a few meters away from the hotel. Radisson Blu Plaza Hotel Oslo is also within walking distance of the Oslo Opera House, Karl Johans gate, and Stortinget.

Radisson Blu Plaza Hotel Oslo Website
https://www.radissonblu.com/en/plazahotel-oslo
Radisson Blu Plaza Hotel Oslo Map
https://goo.gl/maps/gKDsbrHTYcn
Address: Sonja Henies Plass 3, 0185 Oslo
Phone:+47 22 05 80 00

Saga Poshtel Oslo Central

This 2-star hostel is a pleasantly surprising gem located in Kongens Gate 7 in Sentrum. It's a 10-minute walk away from the Oslo Central Station and is strategically located in the city center.

Even with its 2-star accommodations, the hostel nevertheless has a lot to offer its guests including: complimentary Wi-Fi, luggage storage, and 24-hour reception. A communal living room is an excellent place to meet fellow international travelers. The hostel offers guests a buffet breakfast, and it also has a shared kitchen.

Nearby attractions include Stortinget, Karl Johans gate, Nationaltheatret Tram Station, and Aker Brygge.

Saga Poshtel Oslo Central Website
http://www.sagahoteloslocentral.no/
Saga Poshtel Oslo Central Map
https://goo.gl/maps/bC7iHJvfmRK2
Address: Kongens gate 7, 0153 Oslo
Phone:+47 23 10 08 00

The Apartments Company – Parkveien

Located in Parkveien 4, The Apartments Company is a five-minute walk away from the Homansbyen Light Rail Station. It's also a short stroll away from Palace Park, the Royal Palace, and Bislett Stadion.

The Gardermoen airport is 45 minutes away by car, and Nationaltheatret Tram Station is a short walk away. Also within walking distance are the Christiania Theatre, the Nationaltheatret, and the National Museum of Art, Architecture, and Design.

The Apartments Company – Parkveien Website
http://www.theapartmentscompany.no/
The Apartments Company – Parkveien Map
https://goo.gl/maps/3G1pr5pEm10
Address:0195 Oslo, Norway
Phone:+47 22 69 04 50

Thon Hotel Rosenkratz Oslo

This 4-star hotel is located at the Rosenkrantz Gate 1 in Sentrum, and offers a concierge, meeting rooms, and a 24-hour reception. Guests can access a fitness center. The hotel's contemporary rooms include newspapers and wireless Internet access.

There is also a bar and a restaurant where guests can relax after a busy day of touring the Oslo surroundings. From this hotel, you can easily discover the city's best offerings. Thon Hotel Rosenkrantz Oslo is located near the Nationaltheatret, the Oslo City Hall, and the People's Theatre. Oslo Spektrum is a short walk away.

Thon Hotel Rosenkratz Oslo Website
http://www.theapartmentscompany.no/
Thon Hotel Rosenkratz Oslo Map
https://goo.gl/maps/Dgr28RMcQ7N2
Address: Rosenkrantz' gate 1, 0159
Phone:+47 23 31 55 00

6

Top 5 Restaurants

The culinary scene is a Scandinavian gem, and features everything from freshly-caught fish to succulent reindeer. While there are a number of restaurants in the city, listed below are five of the best Oslo restaurants.

Café Engebret

The restaurant is considered the oldest restaurant in Oslo. You get to experience old world charm with draped curtains, wood paneling, and candlelight. The traditional food changes with the seasons, and it's like the food is prepared in a way that is similar to centuries past.

Seafood is served in the spring, reindeer is a constant offering, and fresh cod can be enjoyed in January. While you dine, you can imagine Grieg, Ibsen, and other Nordic greats ate at the restaurant during its 150-year history.

Café Engebret Website
http://engebret-cafe.no/
Café Engebret Map
https://goo.gl/maps/UtPtZSim1LN2
Address: Bankplassen 1
Contact Number: +47 22 82 25 25

Ekebergrestauranten

When visiting Oslo, expect to be entranced by the incomparable vistas and fjords. They are only some of the things that Ekebergrestauranten has to offer. At the restaurant, you can enjoy the beautiful landscapes and Oslo's natural panorama.

You can choose to eat at the veranda, the outdoor restaurant, the café, the private chamber, and the classy dining room. At the restaurant, you are offered the chance to see the majesty of Oslo. You can take in the sights of the glorious city over a quality dish and a glass of wine.

Ekebergrestauranten Website
http://www.ekebergrestauranten.com/

Ekebergrestauranten Map
https://goo.gl/maps/Cvsh7wFv8Xs
Address: Kongsvelen 15
Contact Number: +47 2324 2300

Maaemo

It's not only a restaurant; Maaemo is also a dining experience. The owners suggest that diners allocate an entire evening to appreciate and savor fully the set menu, which is a selection of simplistic reductions and raw foods that add up to 26 plates.

The dining experience can last an entire evening, and wine pairings are chosen carefully to bring out each ingredient's flavor. While spruce juice, reindeer heart, mead gel, and fried rye-bread cream may sound fabricated, they are actually true dishes served in pleasant visual arrangements.

Maaemo Website
https://maaemo.no/
Maaemo Map
https://goo.gl/maps/VsBxHjtXaSA2
Address: Schweigaards gate 15b
Contact Number: +47 9199 4805

Madu

The restaurant is located in the boutique First Hotel Grims Grenka. The restaurant is a traditional Scandinavian restaurant that specializes in seasonal raw food and thrives on the imagination of the chef.

The dishes are cooked at low temperatures or served raw to preserve their subtleties and flavor. The food served loses none of the original goodness and organic nature encased within the ingredients' molecules. The ingredients, mainly seafood and fish, are often smoked, pickled, mixed with contrasting flavors, or cured.

Madu Map
https://goo.gl/maps/hAFG7xARHtj
Address: Kongens gate 5
Contact Number: +47 2310 7200

Markveien Mat og Vinhus

The restaurant chefs use ingredients that are bought from the best local sources. Fresh, locally-grown produce goes into traditional dishes, with lamb, oxtail, and crayfish appearing on the menu. The only thing that makes the ingredients un-Norwegian is the terrine, which is of French origin. The dining room is also of the French style.

Markveien Mat og Vinhus Website
http://www.markveien.no/
Markveien Mat og Vinhus Map
https://goo.gl/maps/S97RP35gt6M2
Address: Torkbajj gate 12
Contact Number: +47 2237 2297

TOP 5 RESTAURANTS

7

Best Famous Oslo City Landmarks

In terms of land area, Oslo is one of the world's largest capital cities. However, only 20 percent of the city's area has been developed; the rest consists of protected forests, parks, numerous lakes, and hills. Open spaces and parks are integral to the cityscape, and can be accessed easily from any part of the city.

The Oslo city center can be explored on foot, as the center has many pedestrian-friendly areas, like Karl Johans gate. Consistently ranked as one of the world's best cities to live in, Oslo is rich in culture and known for its theaters, galleries, and museums. Some of the five best famous Oslo landmarks are listed below.

Aker Brygge

The Aker Brygge area, which is constructed around an abandoned shipyard, is the city's heart and soul. The visually-stunning landmark draws in around 12 million visitors annually. Visitors are drawn by the great restaurants, fine shopping, seafront boardwalk, and patio bars with their fireplaces and snug rugs.

While at Aker Brygge, you can visit the Astrup Fearnley Museum of Modern Art, which houses works by artists Damien Hirst, Jeff Koons, and Andy Warhol, among other contemporary artists.

Location: Bryggegata 9, 0120
Aker Brygge Website
https://www.akerbrygge.no/english/
Aker Brygge Map
https://goo.gl/maps/34yGPqDHRhH2

Akershus Fortress

The fortress rises above the Oslo fjord and sits on the promontory of Akershes. The Akershus Fortress was constructed under the reign of Haakon V. Explore the ramparts and the grounds and then explore the chapel with the tomb of Haakon VII. Also tour the original medieval castle's remains.

Located in the fortress's grounds is the Museum of Norwegian Resistance, and spend a few hours knowing more about the German occupation in Norway during World War II.

Location: Akershus Festning, 0015

Akershus Fortress Website
http://www.forsvarsbygg.no/festningene/Festningene/Akershus-festning/English/
Akershus Fortress Map
https://goo.gl/maps/GNf5MaPSJhH2
Phone:+47 23 09 39 17

Oslo Opera House

With its unique contemporary architecture, the Oslo Opera House is home to the National Opera Theatre and the Norwegian National Opera and Ballet. With its 1,364 seating capacity, the architectural wonder is designed to create the effect that it's slipping into the harbor.

The opera house is also the country's largest cultural building since the 14th century Nidaros Cathedral in Trondheim. As a visitor, you can also join various tours and public programs. Delight also in a stroll on the inclining roof.

Location: Kirsten Flagstads Plass 1, 0150

Oslo Opera House Website
http://operaen.no/
Oslo Opera House Map
https://goo.gl/maps/MULaaQnkcaR2
Phone: +47 21 42 21 21

Royal Palace

Set high on Karl Johans gate's northwest end, the Norwegian Royal Palace is a prominent sight in the city's landscape. The 173-room palace is closed to the public, but visitors can watch the regular changing of the guard on the grounds. They are also free to wander the gardens and grounds. Close by is the Norwegian Nobel Institute.

Location: Bellevue
Royal Palace Website
https://goo.gl/xGLxGD
Royal Palace Map
https://goo.gl/maps/VFt3GQXXyJ92
Phone:+47 22 04 87 00

Vigeland Sculpture Park

The park, which is the largest of its kind in the world, is a famed tourist attraction. The sculpture park, which is open year round, features the works of Gustav Vigeland and contains 650 of his sculptures in wrought iron, granite, and bronze.

In the park, which was completed in 1949, Vigeland took part in the park's layout and design, placing most of the works in five groups along an axis that spans 2,800 feet. The fountain group is the oldest, depicting the human life's cycle.

Location: Nobels gate 32, N-0268

Vigeland Sculpture Park Website
http://www.vigeland.museum.no/no/vigelandsparken
Vigeland Sculpture Park Map
https://goo.gl/maps/GA9s7tjTPPJ2
Phone:+47 23 49 37 00

8

Best Museums

If you love art and you seek to know about cultures other than your own, a visit to Oslo is well worth it, as the city has more than 50 museums. With an art tour of the past and present of Norway's capital, you get to see how Oslo has defined itself as an artistic center in Scandinavia. Below are five of the best museums that the city of Oslo has to offer locals and visitors.

Holmenkollen Ski Museum & Tower

BEST MUSEUMS

As a historical Norwegian landmark, Holmenkollen represents over a century of skiing competitions. Within the ski jump is the Holmenkollen Ski Museum, which presents over four millennia of skiing history.

The museum also showcases exhibitions on modern skiing and snowboarding and Norwegian polar exploration antiquities. On top of the jump tower is the observation deck, which offers sweeping city views. Open year round, the museum also has a shop, café, and ski simulator.

Address: Kongeveien 5, 0787
Phone:+47 916 71 947

Holmenkollen Ski Museum & Tower Website
http://www.skiforeningen.no/holmenkollen
Holmenkollen Ski Museum & Tower Map
https://goo.gl/maps/LDKeg9tcFet

Munch Museum

The museum, also called Munchmuseet, boasts of the world's largest collection of the works of Edvard Munch. The collection provides insight into Munch as an Expressionism pioneer. The artist bequeathed to the city his collection of paintings, drawings, and graphical prints.

Address: Tøyengata 53, 0578
Phone:+47 23 49 35 00

Munch Museum Website
http://munchmuseet.no/
Munch Museum Map
https://goo.gl/maps/FGQwrf5xVf82

National Gallery

Established in 1837, the National Gallery contains Norway's largest public collection of drawings, paintings, and sculpture. The central attractions of the gallery include Edvard Munch's Madonna and The Scream, and paintings by Manet and Cézanne.

The museum's permanent collection highlights works from the Romantic period until the mid-1900s. Other works exhibited are the art of international sculptors and painters. The Fairy Tale Room has art depicting fairy tale creatures like princesses, fairies, and trolls. Admission is free with the Oslo Pass.

Address: Universitetsgata 13, 0164
Phone:+47 21 98 20 00

National Gallery Website
http://www.nasjonalmuseet.no/
National Gallery Map
https://goo.gl/maps/5X2qHiNNKDD2

National Museum − Architecture

The museum explores historical and contemporary themes through photographs, drawings, and models. Designed by Christian Heinrich Grosch, the main building was completed in 1830. After an extension and a renovation by Sverre Fehn, the building started to be used as a museum in 2008.

The building is a juxtaposition of modernist architecture and classicism. It's an encounter between Fehn and Grosch, who are Norway's most important architects of the 20th and 19th centuries, respectively.

Address: Universitetsgata 13, 0164
Phone:+47 21 98 20 00

National Museum – Architecture Website
http://www.nasjonalmuseet.no/
National Museum – Architecture Map
https://goo.gl/maps/F4g9Up3xGFo

The Kon-Tiki Museum

Norwegian ethnographer and adventurer Thor Heyerdahl became famous when, in 1947, he crossed the Pacific Ocean on the Kon-Tiki raft. He then had subsequent expeditions on the reed boats Tigris and Ra.

At the museum, guests can see the original vessels and exhibits on Heyerdahl's expeditions, including Kon-Tiki, Tigris, Ra, Galapagos, Tucume, Fatu-Hiva, Easter Island, Thor Heyerdahl's library, Tiki pop culture, Thor Heyerdahl the person, and underwater exhibit, and a 30-meter cave tour.

Address: Bygdøynesveien 36, 0286
Phone:+47 23 08 67 67

The Kon-Tiki Museum Website
http://www.kon-tiki.no/
The Kon-Tiki Museum Map
https://goo.gl/maps/eFgCb9iDv1G2

9

Best Art Galleries

While Oslo is smaller compared to other international art centers, it's still reputed for its specialist auction houses and galleries. The city's art galleries offer visitors the chance to know more about Norway's art history. They also provide insight for individuals who seek to invest in art while in Oslo.

Astrup Fearnley Museet

The Astrup Fearnley Collection comprises contemporary and modern art that are considered significant in Northern Europe. The museum changes up its collection by rotating exhibits of well-known artists with its permanent collection.

Renowned architect Renzo Piano designed the gallery, and is comprised of 3 pavilions that rest under a uniquely-shaped glass roof. The building is inspired by its maritime environment.

Address: Strandpromenaden 2, 0252
Phone:+47 22 93 60 60

Astrup Fearnley Museet Website
http://www.afmuseet.no/
Astrup Fearnley Museet Map
https://goo.gl/maps/h4Z4U46GbQz

Blomqvist Auction House Gallery

Established in 1870, Blomqvist is the country's largest and oldest auction house. The gallery deals in Norwegian antiques and art, and is considered an Edvard Munch expert.

Aside from paintings, photographs, prints, and sculptures, the gallery also specializes and deals in silver, furniture, china, country antiques, glass, oriental items, and jewelry.

Address: Tordenskiolds gate 5
Phone:+47 22 70 87 70

Blomqvist Auction House Gallery Website
https://www.blomqvist.no/
Blomqvist Auction House Gallery Map
https://goo.gl/maps/fdBCn8sqZtp

Galleri Heer

Galleri Heer was established at its current address in 1986. However, the gallery's history goes back to 1981 when Olav Postmyr opened the gallery in Drøbak.

Galleri Heer is a contemporary art gallery that exhibits the works of various artists: old and young, female and male, and veterans and debutants. The gallery showcases mostly artistic expressions, including photography, drawing, graphics, and sculpture.

Address: Seilduksgata 4, 0553
Phone:+47 22 38 54 32

Galleri Heer Website
http://www.galleriheer.no/
Galleri Heer Map
https://goo.gl/maps/y3GXZ1MdHq62

Museum of Contemporary Art

The Museum of Contemporary Art has four permanent installations, including gallery rooms that are allocated for the works of Louis Bourgeois. The gallery also has a permanent collection of 5,000 works by international and Norwegian artists.

The museum gallery's collection also covers a wide spectrum of media and genres: print-making, paintings, photography, drawing, objects, sculpture, video art, and installation. The gallery offers guided tours in Norwegian every Sunday, and guided tours in English during the summer.

Address: Bankplassen 4, 0151
Phone:+47 21 98 20 00
Museum of Contemporary Art Website
http://www.nasjonalmuseet.no/en/
Museum of Contemporary Art Map
https://goo.gl/maps/kS43YsYTanv

The Queen Joséphine Gallery

The gallery opens during the summer and is open to all Oscarshall visitors. Located in Oscarshall's museum shop annex, the gallery showcases classic Norwegian art.

The gallery is named for Queen Joséphine, who is King Oscar I's mother. Both the king and queen were interested in art, and they laid the groundwork for the classic Norwegian art collection at the Royal Palace today.

Address: Oscarshallveien, 0287
Phone:+47 917 02 361

The Queen Joséphine Gallery Website
http://www.royalcourt.no/artikkel.html?tid=117403
The Queen Joséphine Gallery Map
https://goo.gl/maps/UBLA23fLET62

10

Best Coffee Shops

Oslo has a high standard of living, and residents seek to have the right work-life balance. Oslo's residents also love a good cup of coffee. Below are some of the city's best places to sip a cup of coffee and bite into a delectable pastry.

Alfred

Alfred's head chef, Joni Leskinen, used the success of eco-restaurants as his inspiration for the café. For food preparation, Alfred utilizes only sustainable and locally-sourced produce. Patrons can choose to sit outdoors on the patio or inside the cafe. One of the most highly recommended food items is Alfred's open-faced shrimp sandwich.

Address: Brynjulf Bulls Plass 1, 0250
Phone:+47 400 06 611
Alfred Map
https://goo.gl/maps/VmJukuLwt292

Café Amsterdam

Café Amsterdam is Norway's first Dutch café, and it gives off an authentic Dutch vibe. The café is relaxing and cozy by day, and a dynamic and vibrant pub at night. The artwork and décor all come from the Netherlands, and the traditional snacks let you catch a sneak peek of Dutch cuisine. A must-try dish is bitterballen – a deep fried meatball.

Address: Kristian Augusts Gate 12, 0164
Phone:+47 401 69 089

Café Amsterdam Website
http://cafeamsterdam.no/
Café Amsterdam Map
https://goo.gl/maps/EiJyxJ6Lo8N2

Café Celsius

Café Celsius is your best hangout if you seek an afternoon appreciating Norwegian buildings rich in history. Set in Christiania Square, the café is close to a number of the city's oldest buildings. The vanilla-marinated strawberry is a must-try and the desserts and coffee are outstanding. The outdoor sitting area tends to be crowded during summer.

Address: Rådhusgata 19, 0158
Phone:+47 22 42 45 39
Café Celsius Website
http://www.kafecelsius.no/
Café Celsius Map
https://goo.gl/maps/aiX5E6zXrW72

Grosch

Grosch is a great place to have lunch and it's also a fine venue for hangouts and meetings. Grosch is set right next to the National Museum of Architecture, which was built as Norges Banks in 1828. Guests at Grosch can partake of a relaxing meal beside the historic structure. Some of the recommended desserts served in the café are mousse, waffles, and sweet passionfruit panna cotta.

Address: Bankplassen 3 0151
Phone:+47 22 42 12 12

Grosch Website
http://www.groschbistro.no/
Grosch Map
https://goo.gl/maps/DjHR7ontMpJ2

11

Top 5 Bars

Oslo is known for its relaxing work environment. Moreover, visitors to Oslo can see the sights during the day, and unwind at night. As for locals, they can have a nightcap after a hard day's work. Below are five of the best bars in the city.

Brooms & Hatchets

Brooms & Hatchets offers you an authentic Norwegian way to drink and enjoy a night out. The bar is known to bring out the best in Norwegian culture and identity to its guests. The classy yet modern bar has a superb atmosphere, and the local craftsmanship is showcased flawlessly in the Nordic gastro-pub food and local beers. You can also choose from a variety of spirits and cocktails.

Address: Kongens gate 5, 0153
Phone:+47 23 10 72 00
Brooms & Hatches Website
https://www.facebook.com/broomsandhatchets/

Etoile Bar

Rooftop bars are popular during the summer, and they are an excellent option if you want to enjoy a drink. Set on the Grand Hotel's eighth floor, Etoile Bar allows you to catch a scenic view of the Oslo skyline as well as of Karl Johans gate. At night, the bar becomes vibrant and energetic. The roof terrace is open during good weather.

Address: Karl Johans Gate 31, 0159
Phone:+47 23 21 20 00
Etoile Bar Website
http://www.grand.no/no/restaurantandbar/eight-rooftop-bar.html
Etoile Bar Map
https://goo.gl/maps/XwH1hkJqt3F2

Internasjonalen

Opened in 2003, Internasjonalen is one of the city's best drinking spots. The bar utilizes the functionalist style of Eastern Europe as the décor's main theme, paying homage to the long working class tradition. Internasjonalen serves a variety of wines, snacks, cocktails, and rare spirits. From time to time, live music performances are also held. You can be entertained the entire evening with an eclectic playlist.

Address: Youngstorget 2 A, 0181
Phone:+47 468 25 240
Internasjonalen Website
http://www.internasjonalen.no/
Internasjonalen Map
https://goo.gl/maps/brAhp18Apsv

Izakaya

Izakaya, which is a Japanese pub, offers you a unique drinking experience. The bar brings you a real Japanese drinking experience, as the izakaya culture has been popular in the Asian country for many years. The furnishings and décor stay true to izakaya. Also served are Japanese beers, wines, sake, and spirits.

Address: St. Olavs Gate 7 0165
Phone:+47 463 45 679
Izakaya Website
http://izakayaoslo.com/
Izakaya Map
https://goo.gl/maps/yEMoUThYWxv

Tosca Bar

Tosca Bar, which is set on the Thon Hotel Opera's ground floor, is a popular place to enjoy light drinks and refreshments. Comfortable, colorful chairs paired with exquisite bar tables create a dynamic atmosphere for the bar patrons. Light snacks and small dishes are also served, and many of them are meant to complement your cocktail or glass of wine. Veteran mixologists prepare the cocktails, and you can make your own cocktail, too.

Address: Dronning Eufemias Gate 4, 0191
Phone:+47 24 10 30 00

Tosca Bar Website
https://www.thonhotels.no/hoteller/norge/oslo/thon-hotel-opera/
Tosca Bar Map
https://goo.gl/maps/2j9hXds3uSk

12

Top 5 Nightclubs

Norwegians are usually not big on social drinking. With residents becoming more cosmopolitan, however, Oslo's nightscape continually offers a wider array of nightlife choices. Tourists prefer the British-style pubs, and live jazz has also found its corner. Young professionals are drawn to clubs that let them dance and enjoy listening to live music. Below are 5 of Oslo's top nightclubs.

Blå

Blå is a nightclub for contemporary jazz, live, R&B, hip-hop, and related sounds. It's also a venue that welcomes upcoming acts from around Norway. International artists perform here as well. Concerts are held during the early evenings, while the place turns into a vibrant nightclub well into the night, where Norwegian and international DJs work their magic.

Address: Brenneriveien 9 C, 0182

Blå Website
http://www.blaaoslo.no/kontakt/
Blå Map
https://goo.gl/maps/gbuFiT5WECo

Hard Rock Café Oslo

Hard Rock Café Oslo is a nightclub, bar, and restaurant that fuses contemporary Scandinavian design with vibrant rock n' roll, good food, and classic Hard Rock style. The nightclub and café is open year round, and its walls are covered with famous musicians' rock n' roll memorabilia.

The nightclub and café boasts of more than 30 flat-screens, a stage, and a superb sound system, making it an ideal venue for various events. Moreover, the party atmosphere of the nightclub lasts into the wee hours.

Address: Karl Johans gate 45, 0162
Phone:+47 400 06 260

Hard Rock Café Oslo Website
http://www.hardrockcafe.no/
Hard Rock Café Oslo Map
https://goo.gl/maps/7FbBbCJqLzr

Revolver

This rock arena has a restaurant, a cocktail bar, and a basement bar that holds club nights and concerts. Mission Taco, which is Revolver's restaurant, serves affordable Mexican street food. The bar is open daily and the minimum age to enter is 23 years old. The nightclub's minimum entrance age is 20 years old.

Address: Møllergata 32, 0179
Phone:+47 22 20 22 32

Revolver Website
https://www.revolveroslo.no/
Revolver Map

https://goo.gl/maps/KSymx1TVMXk

Skaugum

At Skaugum's special atmosphere, you get to enjoy good music and a proper backyard. Open year round, Skaugum offers shade during summers and heating cables, heat lamps, hot drinks, an open grill, and dancing during colder days.

The unique nightclub has 3 floors, with 50 sinks bolted to walls and an unexpected music profile. Concerts are regularly held during summers. Concerts are also held at the bar year round. Skaugum is also a popular weekend nightclub, attracting guests from around town.

Address: Solligata 2, 0254
Phone: +47 23 13 11 40

Skaugum Website
http://palacegrill.no/
Skaugum Map
https://goo.gl/maps/8Gj74MikBPL2

The Villa

The Villa is an electronica club that is highly rated among its guests. The nightclub plays underground music like techno, house, drum 'n' bass, dubstep, electro, and other musical genres.

The nightclub consists of two dance floors. The weekends feature international and Norwegian DJs, artists, and live acts. Guests have to be at least 23 years old to enter the nightclub. However, guests 20-22 years of age may be able to enter so long as they send a prior email to the club.

Address: Møllergata 23, 0179
Phone:+47 932 55 745

The Villa Website
http://www.thevilla.no/
The Villa Map
https://goo.gl/maps/ynJ6qVUj2XQ2

13

Unique or Special Activities You can do Only in Oslo

Oslo is indeed of the world's most beautiful cities. It's also a great place to know more about and experience Nordic culture. Moreover, there are also a few things that can only be experienced in Oslo. Below are some of the unique things, underground activities, alternative sights, and hidden gems that you can enjoy.

Flea Markets

If you want a unique and authentic Oslo experience, it's a good idea to go to a thrift shop or flea market. The city has at least seven flea markets, but the most recommended go-to markets are Blå and Birkelunden flea market.

Birkelunden sells mainly vintage books, jewelry, and furniture. Blå sells second-hand items and handicrafts like glass, ceramics, paintings, bags, and wool. Here, you can also meet the local designers and artists, and their inspiring artistic perception.

Notable Flea Market Addresses:
Brenneriveien 9 C, 0182
https://goo.gl/maps/epp5ZciCuLJ2
Grünerløkka 0552
https://goo.gl/maps/uX7BB6xq7K82

Music Festivals

Concert venues are everywhere, as Norwegians love their local and international music. Oslo's largest music festival is Øya Festival, which takes place yearly during August. The festival attracts over 60,000 music lovers to Medieval Park.

If you can't chance upon the Øya Festival, there are other spectacular live music performances in the city. Mono, Blå, and Rockefeller have the most cutting-edge sound systems and the more popular bands.

Here, you can enjoy listening to folk music or heavy metal:

Blå
Address:Brenneriveien 9, 0182
Blå Website
http://www.blaaoslo.no/kontakt/

Bla Map
https://goo.gl/maps/dr7NyG3dwT72

Mono
Address: Pløens Gate 4, 0181
Mono Website
http://www.cafemono.no/
Mono Map
https://goo.gl/maps/pPurYmKUHsR2

Rockefeller
Address:Torggata 16, 0181
Rockefeller Website
http://www.rockefeller.no/
Rockefeller Map
https://goo.gl/maps/Egn3sogH2SN2

Norwegian Architecture

Architecture enthusiasts would find Oslo a paradise. Norwegian architecture's new direction has dramatically changed the city's landscape. From modern styles to medieval structures, there are many buildings that are worth a visit. Futuristic streamlined designs characterize the Holmenkollen Ski Jump and ZipLine. The unique Mortensrud Church integrates nature with slate glass.

Notable Architecture:

Mortensrud Website
https://kirken.no/kirkeneioslo
Mortensrud Church Map
https://goo.gl/maps/fTnv5bkhiP72
Address:Helga Vaneks vei 15, 1281
Phone:+47 23 62 99 80

Holmenkollen Ski Jump and ZipLine Website
http://www.skiforeningen.no/holmenkollen
Holmenkollen Ski Jump and ZipLine Map
https://goo.gl/maps/FviCwbLiMgA2
Address: Kongeveien 5, 0787
Phone:+47 22 92 32 00

Østmarka Wilderness Area

Østmarka, which is set east of Oslo, is unique as its vegetation and geology are markedly different from other forests in the surroundings.

During summer, you can go biking, hiking, and swimming or fishing in the lake. You can also delight in some of the Arctic animals and plants. During winter, you can watch the aurora borealis that skirts the city or ski on the trails. At Østmarka, you get to appreciate Oslo's priceless beauty.

Location: Østmarka, 0687

Østmarka Wilderness Area Map
https://goo.gl/maps/AQqEPxqt95o

Street Art

Graffiti, murals, and paintings can be found all over Oslo. You can find art in a wall's tiny corner next to a garbage bin. Street art may entirely cover a building's whole wall. There are also artists working on street art projects.

Oslo-based artists Pøbel and Dolk, for example, have worked on the 'Living Decay' project, which pertains to a derelict house in the Lofoten Archipelago.

14

Safety While Traveling in Oslo

When you visit Oslo, you are guaranteed of your safety. However, you shouldn't let your guard down and throw caution to the wind. Anything can still happen, and you still must take precautions when going to another country.

Generally, crimes against tourists in Oslo and the rest of Norway are rare, and crime rates are normally low. Crimes that involve violence are somewhat unheard of. Public transport that is generally used by tourists is deemed safe. It's common sense, though, to keep an eye on your valuables in crowded areas in order to prevent problems that might occur.

A reason that Oslo may be safe can be attributed to the longer daylight hours. During the busy summer travel months, it's only dark between 12 midnight and 4 in the morning. During the darker hours, even a bit of light can still filter through. It is agreed in general that crime is likely to happen during the dark, which is not a conducive factor in the city.

Not all places in the city are tourist-friendly, though. You may want to steer clear of the area west/south of the Central Station. The area is deemed to be the city's drug-dealing sector. It's also considered the city's seedier area. While that area is normally safe, you don't have to go there if you don't have a specific reason.

Since 2009, prostitution has been declared illegal in Norway.
Oslo has excellent hygiene and health standards. You can drink the tap water, which is considered high quality.

Phone Police:112
Phone Ambulance:113

15

3-Day Travel Itinerary

Oslo is a paradox – a city set in the countryside. While Oslo is one of the largest European capitals in terms of land area (450 square kilometers), its population is quite small – with only 1.5 million inhabitants.

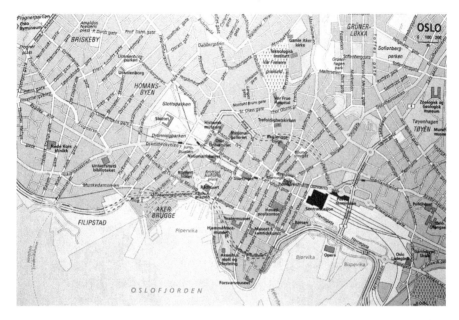

Thus, if you have enjoyed the shops, galleries, cafes, and bars, you can easily slip on to a train or bicycle, into a kayak or yacht, or into ice skates or skis and explore the great outdoors. You can do that without leaving Oslo's land area. Below is one suggested itinerary that lets you explore the rural and urban area of Oslo in three days.

Oslo Kayak Tours Website
http://www.oslokayaktours.no/
Phone: +47 95368249

First Day: Exploring Oslo by Land

Oslo was established in 1048, and razed to the ground in 1624. Because of the natural and man-made changes that were done to the city, modern-day Oslo is now an eclectic mix of new and old culture and architecture. Oslo is the city that inspired Edvard Munch the artist and Henrik Ibsen the playwright.

Start your day by feeling this cultural and diverse city on a sightseeing tour. Go to the land-based city museums and know more about Viking history. Also visit the art galleries and folk museums. A must-see attraction is the Vigeland Sculpture Park.

Second Day: Exploring Oslo by Sea

Oslo is situated at the Oslo Fjord's head. Ride a ferry boat and take in the vibrant scenery. Enjoy looking at the inlets, islands, and the Akershus Fortress that had once defended the city from foreign attacks.

If you want to explore Oslo by land and sea, take the bus/boat tour that includes the maritime museum. Go for the Oslo experience if you want to see the museums, fjords, the Holmenkollen Ski Jump, and the Kon-Tiki Raft. With this tour, you get to experience the countryside, fjord, and city in one go.

Third Day: Exploring Oslo in Detail

Contemporary Oslo has a lot to offer you if you seek the time to enjoy the sights. Board the Hop-On, Hop-Off Bus and take a look at the cosmopolitan city's shops and cafes. You can also pretend to be a Viking and visit the Viking Ship Museum.

You can also go to the Nobel Peace Centre and commemorate the achievements of individuals who seek to make the world a better place. You can also visit the Munch Museum and see the works of Norway's most famous painter.

3-DAY TRAVEL ITINERARY

Nobel Peace Center Website
https://www.nobelpeacecenter.org/en/
Nobel Peace Center Map
https://goo.gl/maps/Khiy9SzuH9E2
Phone:+47 48 30 10 00

With the Oslo Pass, you can access 33 attractions and museums. As the sun sets, you can take a cruise on a conventional wooden ship and imagine you're Thor Heyerdahl.

Here's another three-day itinerary.

First Day

Buy shrimp off the shrimp boats at the harbor fronting the town hall (Rådhus), and ride a ferry over to the Bygdøy peninsula, which houses some of the city's major museums that are within walking distance of each other.

Explore Fram (the polar ship), the Viking ships, the Norwegian Maritime Museum, the Norwegian Folk Museum, and the Kon-Tiki Museum. In the afternoon, visit the Vigeland Sculpture Park in Frognerpark.

Second Day

Use this day for the Frommer's walking tour, and enjoy your lunch at a traditional Norwegian restaurant. Visit the Edvard Munch Museum in the afternoon. During summer, indulge in some fresh air and beer at the Studenter Lunden, which is close to the National Theatre.

Third Day

In the morning, take another Frommer's walking tour, and have lunch along your tour. After lunch, tour the Akershus Fortress and the nearby Norwegian Resistance Museum.

Late in the afternoon, go to the Tryvannstårnet lookout tower and the Holmenkollen Ski Museum, where you can enjoy sweeping Oslo views. You can also eat dinner at Holmenkollen.

--

Indeed, Oslo is a wonderful city that has it all: winter and summer, outdoor and indoor, sea and land. Your only concern is that how you'll explore the city in just three days.

16

Conclusion

I want to thank you for reading this book! I sincerely hope that you received value from it!

If you received value from this book, I want to ask you for a favour. Would you be kind enough to leave a review for this book on Amazon?

Ó Copyright 2017 by Gary Jones - All rights reserved.

This document is geared towards providing exact and reliable information in regards to the topic and issue covered. The publication is sold with the idea that the publisher is not required to render accounting, officially permitted, or otherwise, qualified services. If advice is necessary, legal or professional, a practiced individual in the profession should be ordered.

- From a Declaration of Principles which was accepted and approved equally by a Committee of the American Bar Association and a Committee of Publishers and Associations.

In no way is it legal to reproduce, duplicate, or transmit any part of this document in either electronic means or in printed format. Recording of this publication is strictly prohibited and any storage of this document is not allowed unless with written permission from the publisher. All rights reserved.

The information provided herein is stated to be truthful and consistent, in that any liability, in terms of inattention or otherwise, by any usage or abuse of any policies, processes, or directions contained within is the solitary and utter responsibility of the recipient reader. Under no circumstances will any legal responsibility or blame be held against the publisher for any reparation, damages, or monetary loss due to the information herein, either directly or indirectly.

Respective authors own all copyrights not held by the publisher.

The information herein is offered for informational purposes solely, and is universal as so. The presentation of the information is without contract or any type of guarantee assurance.

The trademarks that are used are without any consent, and the publication of the trademark is without permission or backing by the trademark owner. All trademarks and brands within this book are for clarifying purposes only and are the owned by the owners themselves, not affiliated with this document.

Made in United States
Orlando, FL
29 June 2025